WHEN THE BARBARIANS ARRIVE

Alvin Pang

WHEN THE BARBARIANS ARRIVE

2012

Published by Arc Publications
Nanholme Mill, Shaw Wood Road
Todmorden OL14 6DA, UK
www.arcpublications.co.uk

Design by Tony Ward

978 1906570 98 9 (pbk)
978 1906570 99 6 (hbk)
978 1908376 33 6 (ebook)

Cover image:
Detail from 'Book IV / X: Centre of Dependency'
from 'The Consolations of Museology' (2008)
by Michael Lee (Singapore).
Copyright © Michael Lee, 2008,
by kind permission of the artist.
http://michaellee.sg/#11

International Editor: John Kinsella

CONTENTS

for Fong Hoe Fang,
pioneer, boss-man, hero, friend

INITIATION

My father taught me how to toss a line.
He rigged up the reel by thumbing
screws, stretched line like a nerve
through the narrowing
circles of the rod, gave it a quick twist
and the hook was on, curved like a
question, poignant and dangling.

I groped the supple rod, trembling in my hands, feeling
the sway and dip of it. He worked
a secret ritual with his hands, pierced unflinching
some shrimp or small fry pinched near the tail
painlessly, left it to twirl in its throes, twitching.

Or, casting for another batch,
he would clutch the ocean in a fistful of drag.
As children we would crowd round to watch
the magic hiss and hop of his net, upbeach.
When he unfolded the petals of his catch

we would wrestle like fish after fry
to taste the sea in the fresh, well
scalded shrimp – just arrived, alive, now
new within us – although
we kept our distance, lest we mar the spell.

For my first fling he chose a shrimp. 'Thick
and sweet' he said, 'to take the big ones.'
It jerked as we rehearsed the ritual

drawback and right flick,
then patted me off to jostle
the men, find a place of mine,
squeeze in a spot to toss in my own line.

FLY-FISHING

A soft flick, vague as memory,
and then the straight plunge

of weight, laying out a line from
life to life, a morse-code of motion.

You listen for the slips, the signal,
the tentative nudge, and count

each wink in flaked sunlight
a trout for every thought. One

slapped the river in a frenzy of thrashing
then flashed away, lure and not

steel in its dark maws. But
the joy is in the tense tremble,

the reining in with the reel
held close to your ear, watching

the vague wake burst
into rich silvery form. Later,

stooped to scale it and oblivious
to the wet slime slick on my skin,

I might remember leaping gurgle oracles,
bubbles babbled like words, recalling

men back to the bait
with caution and exuberance:

immerse yourself and play by the rules.

FRICTION

I

Tending to her, I run my hands
down the papyrus of her skin,
I rub away at the bruises,
where the veins had been
scrawled on too long
by the drip needle, have spilled
their blue in dull pools
beneath her skin.

They fascinate my touch –
small, soft circles
from which warmth begins
to spread, as dead blood
disperses, and feeling
returns.

I imagine her
gaunt cheeks, soft hollow
fill and breathe with colour,
her eyes catching fire
as I rub at her wrists
for the heat of friction.

II

I remember what my grandfather did
when I ran out of the shower and slipped
and nearly broke my head on the wall.

He bore me on his back like a gunny
sack all the way to hospital, despite being ill,
and waited in the silent corridors until

they were sure I was fine. I remember – but this
is what grandmother would tell me,
over and over, as I flinched, ungrateful

with pain as she tended my bruises
with firm thumb and the soft balm of story,
the next time I fell, and the next time.

THE SCENT OF THE REAL

For Cyril, who said:
     'Real life, if there is a real life, is boring, and therefore, not art.'

Of course it isn't.
But there's that
one second between
dreaming and waking
when we can never be
too sure where
and which we are.

Now and then it follows us
into the bare room
of consciousness;
blanket sagged to floor
again, the bed wincing
in its regular creak.

With luck, there's someone
beside you, who doesn't notice
the slight glaze in your eye,
a fracture of the light
not attributed to lust, for once.

Go back to sleep,
you say, stroking
the oiled finery of his hair.
Or you locate
the fulcrum of his breathing,
unbalance him with the point
of a kiss, so you both fall
into a sea of your own making,
riding its extraordinary tide.

Even in the throes
of receiving
and expelling air
in quickening lapses
you succumb
to an unerotic prescience.

Already you envision
the harried buttoning,
frantic rush to road,
a claustrophobia of routine.
Lifted from one sweet immersion
to drown in another.

By now so far gone
into the commonplace
you've forgotten the shore
and shape of love,

the body's familiar narratives
retold in every touch, aching
for touch, two dying
creatures seeking equal ballast
in desire's mirror.

How many times
will you hear this story
in the quiet keeping of strangers
whose hearts you cannot know
but through the glass
of your own hunger?

As if the scent of the real
is simply found, and not
with each hour's singular musk
diffused, unmarked, into sunlight.

As if to bear clear witness
to your longing alone
isn't the only art
there is.

HOMECOMING

On that day the tide will turn
and softly bring its crested head
to rest on the cheek of shore.

The jambu tree will shed
moist leaves, returning to earth
its debt of tears.

Every cloud will move
into its chosen place. Even the sun
will understand their boldness.

For so long I have listened to the call
of mountains in their loneliness,
the river's thirst to follow ocean.

I know the years trapped in you
like so many birds, their wings
the very flutter of your heart.

At that hour, I will uncage
your body's sadness with my own,
and make the sound locks make

springing open.

SHADES OF LIGHT IN HOLLAND VILLAGE

Say you just got a raise. The last good kiss
you'll remember for life is waiting to happen,
but you come here – Friday night, Saturday night –
the mock Latino bars that didn't last, bars that did,
cafes and coffee-shops that keep up.
The magazine stall on the corner must have turned thirty,
the proprietors still furtively fingering
glossy foreign magazines like contraband.

What they're really selling now
is ease. People come for love of mess, looking for a stab
of feeling, the suddenness of pain, any kind of intoxication.
Well-kept bodies who leave each year
more regretful than the last. Running from silence
into noise. Even the rooftop Balinese illusion of Café 211,
four storeys above ground, can't hide their boredom.

Isn't this the life? That languorous drowning of the senses?
Isn't this defeat so subtle, our bohemian afterlife,
token as a piece of heaven, resounding in seclusion,
all the world will let you have
until the hunger you came from
dies from inside?

Say no to yourself. The old man on the void deck,
already forty when these streets were laid, still laughs
although his legs have jumped ship. Some night soon,
he says, I'll turn off the lights in my room
and never see the sun again. You tell him no
in your head. The taxi that brought you here
is still out there, running for what it's worth

to hunt down the kind of money
you can't even buy lunch with; your fatigue
and unclaimed grief mark the air with sighs
disguised as breathing, and it will kill you one day
no matter what you do.
      So the struggle now is with the stiff
bolt on your front door, the stubborn wilting
of your balcony ferns, the straining of your neck
to catch one glimpse of the woman who loves you
in the best possible light.

WHAT TO WRITE ABOUT IN COLD STORAGE, CIRCA 2000 AD

Half-asleep, and holding the red earth of here and now
close at hand, it is easier to walk past the battlefield that is
real grass into the cool shade of track lighting, reconditioned
air hinting at just the right scent of harvest time, bouquet of
    peaches,
fresh lime with an aftertaste of new apples. Reminds you of
    autumn,
if you've ever known such a thing as leaves dying into colour
and fruit bursting their seams like dresses shrunken from the wash,
like prisoners given amnesty for an hour choosing art over hunger.
The idea of choice, need turned into gold. Sail past the verdant
    aisles
of kai lan, dou miao, basil, asparagus, beet. Ponder the
    introversion
of mushrooms, the luscious enticement of tomatoes, firm grip
and fullness of ripe flesh. Pick a pasta, any pasta, their cryptic
labels slip your tongue as easily as Latin, finger the cheeses, how
any civilisation could think of eating mouldy curds
and at these prices. Finish off at the billboard:
lost pet, spare kittens, maid seeks expat family, garage sale,
english tuition, native speaker, results guaranteed.

And you tell me there's nothing to write about, that life
has handed you a blank sheet and you're just waiting in line
to pay up and get out. You could even be right. Maybe this is
all there is: moving on, moving up, a queue line
of souls waiting for checkout and proceeding to wherever.
The cash register bleats its numbers into view, there's
the sudden sharp smell of fresh money changing hands, plastic
bags rustling frantically to be on their way.
Or this could be nothing at all, backdrop against which
you ought to scrawl a life less ordinary, dress down,

get your hands dirty in the real stuff. Bloody your fists
against the hard edges of the world. Think deep thoughts.
Change the world. Get a life. Well,
your car's parked outside, here's the shopping and the keys,
when you're done come upstairs – dinner's at seven.

WHAT IT MEANS TO BE LANDLESS

When I look out the window I can only see cloud
and the top of other people's roofs. Gardens
are out of reach, even the smallest blade of grass.
In stormy weather rain dashes right past me
on the way to somewhere thirsty.
It means shade. It means the herbs and spices
I try to cultivate wilt under fluorescent lighting
and air conditioning. It means safety. It means
clean hands. It means I taste old tin,
sodium benzoate, vacuum sealed meats
when the market is closed. I can have
whatever I want as long as it's something on offer.
I can give you an address that in fifty years
will not even be memories of a lost childhood.
When I travel, I look for floodplains and unscalable
mountains, for the small scruffed kittens
scratching at litter and soil and fresh greens
we eat later not knowing where they came from.
It means I will be burned, not buried. It means I am
the son of no soil. It means I have no fear of
droughts and bandits, of hard work, and children
at play have earth brushed away from their knees
in case it makes them sick. It means enough,
and nothing and smiling, every morning as I rise,
the puzzled smile of the long asleep.

ABSENCES

Taman Serasi

Cluny to widen:
an eating place is eaten
by road, of all things.

Paya Lebar Primary

Uprooted, literally
by the subterranean wrecking crew
of raintree, angsana, flame of the forest
which were of course
the next to go.

Yew Court

It is when I ponder these facades
that I know our city is corrupt
in meaning, its intent
revision, not remembrance.

Hong Lim

There are more eyes in this island of park
than will look upon your failures
and you call that prosperity.

Merlion

But you are not going
to be removed after all, merely
have your view restricted for a while,
until they finally put you
where you can be watched
at all times.

POEM FOR AN ENGINEER

This poem has no intention of changing the world
or even moving it one iota. For that you need
a more exact science: aeronautics, civil engineering.
You need plenty of expertise, money, management,
countless nights redrafting plans in the lonely grove
of your cubicle. While you calculate angles, calibrate
cross-shafts and supporting structures, your wife
has fallen away into sleep, your dog beguiled
by the slow wheeling of the moon on its careless axis.
This is serious work. What do poems know about
the imperatives of balance and stress, the calculus
of load-bearing metres? This one spent its childhood
dissecting sonnets, as you grazed, in the class
next door, on vast plains of lines and numbers.
While you struggled with compass and slide rule,
it was dividing dactyls from iambs, dreaming up
wild rivers, airborne castles, towers kissing sky.

Not for you, whose shoulder is to the hard stone
of this life, whose idea of sleep is one long dull
ache in the back of the neck you cannot reach.
But you are almost done. You check the figures
one last time, as the poem watches, innumerate
and invisible. Finishing for the night, gifting
schematics to the unmagical gloom; straight
lines on paper that will one day become a bridge,
a skyscraper, a lighter-than-air miracle.

MERLIGN

Even though there are more
websites on you than verses;
even though you evoke
cameras more than pride,
postcards more than praise;
even though your titan child
is now terrorising history and
small children on Sentosa.

Still you seem to have a face poets love
to woo. There was the old gentleman,
windswept, seablown, wandering home
with a suitcase of dreams, who
treated you like a queen, hoping
to press you for secrets.

And then the lady with thick glasses,
who thought she saw Ezekiel's cherubim,
the *sign episteme* of higher forces
forever barring the way to paradise.

And that young man, himself half lion,
with barbed tale raised, words coiled
like a fist. Eyes louder than silence.

Still others, perplexed
as much by your blank stare
as their maddening need to know,
burden you with the fret
of lost causes and years of waiting,

become now the need
to apostrophise what is rock
to make it bear weight.
How we wallow in metaphors!

As a child I walked through a garden
to gawk at you, a giant too tall
for a child's mind to wrap around.
Risking the simplest of pleasures:
a closer glance, a furtive stroke,
reaching for scale and contact –

and now, as a man, forever measuring shadows.

No need to go on with this pretence,
these riddles and voices. This is a heap
of fashioned stone, too light to carry souls.

Rough beast, you are neither idol nor ideal.
Your heart is hollow, cold, and open
for admission, but we have nowhere else
to hide our dreams. Take what names

we have to give, and hold our secrets well.
Keep what matters and what counts.
The rest you can spit as spray.

"By night, The Merlion awakens during a spectacular light, sound and water show extravaganza. The 'Rise of the Merlion' will be staged three times a night. Colour lasers will shoot from the eyes of the Merlion and from the Musical Fountain in synchronisation with the symphony of dancing water fountains in a 15-minute show designed to be a crowd-pleaser."

The Sentosa Homepage

"In the park people see Merlion from behind, so most visitors
gather across the river."

Japanese Website

"Perhaps having dealt in things, / Surfeited on them, / Their spirits yearn again
for images"

'Ulysses by the Merlion', EDWIN THUMBOO

"… O feckless wanderer / remember to respect my creators."

'The Merlion to Ulysses', LEE TZU PHENG

"I still do wish it had paws."

'The Merlion', ALFIAN SA'AT

THE MEANING OF WEALTH IN THE NEW ECONOMY

"Wealth… is the means by which we fulfill our desires."
Interview with STAN DAVIS & CHRIS MEYERS,
Harvard Business School Publishing

Hence the cat's languid stretch, its bullet spring, the puppy
eyes of the one you love, asking undue favours
you resent, yet relent to. The mercenary burst
of bougainvillea, machine-gun clatter of rubber-seeds falling
to hard ground as December comes, bearing fistfuls of rain.
Consider the lilies of the field, how like your pale hunger,
the hollow in the gut that pulls you forward, the lust
to work, earn, mate, the same gravity that binds
water to sky, impels birds to song and blood, both.

Remember the electric twitch of a nerve
as skin kissed skin for the first time ever?
Every word you waste in trade for half-truths
you need to get by, turning the volume down on guilt
as you come home past midnight, head bowed, rehearsing
lies, as you knock on the door. Every lapse in your wellness
diet, stolen Oreos, prophylactic silences, each step you take
away from the home of your childhood, thirsting for road.

Nothing but riches, between the leafy congregation of trees
and the echo of a single prayer down empty aisles, as
cars slam in unison and grumble one by one into gear.
A child's gurgle and squeal, the kind that brings parents running
for a glimpse of joy, reward, and willing to pay for it with
love. In which case we have always known this bounty, the means
to open a window and let the morning in for all it's worth.

You hoard a little every time you put aside, in sleep,
your daily dying. The doubling, and doubling again of years
of weight, of sorrow, that longing, for the one thing
you know you can never have, which keeps you alive.
In your dreams of being free, everything you've always wanted
to be, you walk smiling and whole, away
from the infinite riches of the world.

OTHER THINGS

> "To plant a garden is to believe in tomorrow."
>
> AMANA COLONY, IOWA

To buy a potted plant is to admit both faithlessness and need. To water the plant, perhaps daily, perhaps once in a while when you remember and the leaves start to droop, is as close to love as it gets.

Other things mean other things.

To light a lamp is to hide darkness in the same closet as sleep, along with silence, desire, and yesterday's obsessions. To read a book is to marry two solitudes, the way a conversation erases and erects, words prepare for wordlessness, a cloud for its own absence, and snow undresses for spring.

The bedroom is where you left it, although the creases and humps on the sheets no longer share your outline and worldview. In that way, they are like the children you never had time for.

A cooking pot asks the difficult questions: what will burn and for how long and to what end.

TV comes from the devil who comes from god who comes and goes as he pleases. To hide the remote control in someone's house is clearly a sin, but to take the wrong umbrella home is merely human.

The phone is too white to be taunting you. The door you shut stays shut. The night is reason enough for tomorrow, whatever you believe.

Remember, the car keys will be there after the dance. Walls hold peace as much as distance. A kettle is not reason enough for tears.

The correct answer to a mirror is always, yes.

At 9 he planted a clutch of seed blooms, carefully observed their daily frenzy.

At 22 he began recording the story of the river which ran behind his house, down from the foothills of a nearby mountain and on to the distant ocean. It told him everything he asked of it and more, eagerly and without pause, until the winter months when it finally withdrew, spent and dry mouthed, to the mountains to sleep.

He wrote down all he had heard in long cursive script that meandered across the page.

He had time and was alone, and the fire was well-fed with wood from the surrounding forests, whose tale he also collected, when he was 30.

At 46 he started a biography of the wind, who'd often peek over his shoulder while he worked by the water's edge. Not until he was 54 did he catch her often enough to probe and grasp her deeper impulses.

By the time he turned 63 he was ready to begin his memoirs. It was of course going to be his most difficult work. People lived so fiercely, he was said to remark, at times as if they could cease to be at any moment, or otherwise as if they were going to be around forever.

No one knew what happened to the final manuscript. Critics who had seen his work in progress described it as a chronicle of history through the eyes of the forgotten. By now he had many imitators as well as detractors, many of whom were once admirers who gave up waiting for him to complete each work.

Years after his death at the age of 110, someone recognised his true magnum opus: a carefully pruned pattern of ash, dew, footsteps and flowering trees in the shape of a single haiku, imprinted on the land where he used to live, visible only from the heavens.

SALT

> "But his wife, from behind him, looked back,
> and she became a pillar of salt."

Genesis 19:26

He was one of those who pushes on
at any cost, his eyes ever on the future.
Thinking of the next coin and bed,
a place to stow us for the night.
Not one to look back, that man.
Ready to offer his daughters
as a bribe for peace. His own little girls.

Still, a good husband. Stayed out
of the way at home, mostly.
Helped fetch water from the well
when she was with child. Even wove her
baskets once: lopsided, childish efforts –
you'd expect that from a man – which she kept
on the shelf by the altar. And once or twice
in his passion he'd call out her name, her name.

He was a lover of the old stories,
how they urge us to succour all who come
under our roofs. The night it happened
he was telling us about his childhood,
how he would catch locusts from the fields,
trap their wings' seething in clay pots,
his small hands containing whirlwinds.
I've watched him teach his young son
the same trick, the desert sun touching
his white hair with passing gold. His
fissured skin, its smell of wet rushes.

More and more I think she figured even then.
That she did it on purpose, we have no doubt.
Said nothing when he gave us to the mob.
Made ready in silence, that small mouth we share
a tight, thin line aimed nightward.
It would have been her breed of love:
to be the one left behind, clearing space
for nations to come. Or at least an ending
she could choose, a sudden white escape.

That night my father called for wine
within sight of our city's cinders, face to
the wind's raw sting, his cheeks salting over.
The rest you know. I visit her sometimes
although the years have worn her, unkindly.
I do not bring my son. I do not touch her.

I can see what she means
by that blank stare, the slump of her neck,
the frozen curse she has become. None of us
will ever be clean again, she knew, the night
her back turned towards us as we climbed.

AUBADE

"My love, I fear the silence of your hands."

MAHMOUD DARWISH

Overnight, my heart, the forest has grown cold
and every leaf shivers with the sure knowledge of its fall,
shivers yellow and maple-red and mauve, summer remembered
in vermillion dying. When I walk the river now

it bears merely the lightest press of feet, my body swaying
to keep balance in the whetted breeze. I had to leave you
on the absent shore, a warm bloom nesting in the reeds,
an unfixed, iridescent eye. How we part

only the morning knows, and what we said already dew.
Tomorrow after tomorrow we will find the tongue to
remember our silences, or borrow words from the night's
vocabulary of sighs. Grief will teach you new names

and I will answer, hollow, in drumbeats and echoes,
in footsteps and softly closed doors, never looking
at you, never back. I place these words now in the vault
of sleep before it comes. Before the burial and the blood.

THE BURNING ROOM

Aubade on a picture of spontaneous combustion

When my lover returns
to his wife, his suburban apartment, the comfort
of a seasoned bed bearing
his beautiful weight

I say nothing.
I do not nod nor sigh nor breathe the light
starting to bleed into the room
the colour of saints

being martyred in portraits.
I walk the gallery of his absence, a tourist only
to this surfeit of space,
the erasure of lines

that is his gift to me.
It is enough, I think, to watch over the wide
territory of his need, to guard
the frontiers of desire

with my body and silence.
It is enough. And so I do not stir,
even when the flames bloom
fresh petals

from my unbrushed hair,
pursed eyelids. I disappear
into photographic retreat,
chemical shadow. So

when my lover returns
I am already the ash he wonders at
and brushes gently away
from the hood of his car.

INCENDIUM AMORIS

"Burning incense could cause cancer according to a scientific study conducted by researchers from Taiwan, who found high levels of carcinogens in the smoke of incense burned in Buddhist temples."

Associated Press (2 Aug 2001)

"I have groped my breast seeking whether this burning were from any bodily cause outwardly. But when I knew that it was only kindled inwardly from a ghostly cause, and that this burning was nought of fleshly love or concupiscence, in this I conceived it was the gift of my Maker."

Richard Rolle, *The Fire of Love* (14th C)

I

Now we know our prayers
are killing us. Offer incense, set flame
to sandalwood, give your soul
to the votive glow of oil lamp and candle;
all it summons is this secret bird of prey,
silence fluttering beneath the rib-cage.
So the slow burn towards divinity
begins from within, after all: ashes to ashes,
flesh expiring from smoke into grace.
Gather enough faith
and it could kill a city.

II

We sensed the bigger picture that day
on Jurong Island: refineries humming
like desert temples; land gathered and burnt
for one purpose only. On the horizon
smokestacks tower like Seventh Month joss,

under whose gaze even light wavers,
cowed into sunset. Second after second
the waste flares roar
their fierce syllable of
love
love
love

III

How often we fall to the naked gaze of fire,
trusting the blaze of fact, faith, desire
to light the way out from ourselves to wholeness.
As if salvation is earned by becoming less,
by feeding our dreams to the right combustion.
Does the soul hide in plasma? Is God a question?
The unsolved science of this calculable space,
whose name resides in the geometry of light?
Perhaps freedom gleams in answers which escape
us, eludes our sense of what could be. In which case
we are more than what a quantity of ash might
hold, and what we seem to lose, released from shape
only. Any day soon, we could stumble on paradise
in the embers of here and now, and what we sacrifice.

CANDLES

oi, ah pa know you take candle from the church again, you going to get it.

nevermind i bring them back when you study finish. you dont say he dont know. so dark how to read, how to study?

got moon tonight can see a bit. ah leong house got light, i use mirror can borrow a bit of light. good enough. candle you bring back. i dont want wait get scolding because of you.

i bring all the way home you ask me to bring back for what? anyway tonight good friday church got so many candles they where got notice nine less?

notice dont notice also wrong. you bring them back.

dont want.

go now. late already, wait ah pa come home you die.

dont want. wait the sisters see me bring back so many candles they know i took them.

just say you give them to baby jesus lor.

so stupid, baby jesus is christmas lah. good friday is dead jesus!

anything lah. i not go church one how i know? you just bring them back there ok? ah pa always say people must be honest. cannot steal, cannot cheat, cannot lie.

ah pa say that but he also lie what. last week health inspector come he also lie, say our house very clean. actually he hide two dead cockroach under one shoe.

that was different. that was government. lie to government dont count because they dont care whether you good or bad, they just want money for licence. no license we die they where got care.

jesus also like government what. he where got care whether you blind or not, house got light or not. he just hang up there all day for people to see, put money in box, give him so many candles for nothing. he also not taking exam, i borrow some candles to study why cannot.

aiya up to you lah. say so much also no use. you better go study before ah pa come home.

say so much i hungry already. i go downstairs buy mee from Fat Girl, you want?

dont want, i full. ah ma see you eat some more she scold you. eat and eat, so stubborn and fat like pig. wait you dont study fail exam then you know. you so fat and stubborn next time can do what?

i can be driver like ah pa, or sell meat like ah leong, or gangster like ah soon. then government come ask for money i call my gang beat them up. anyone bully you or sis i beat them up.

xiao, you become gangster get injured how? head kena parang chop one big hole how?

then you better quick study become doctor lah. then if i need hospital
you can cure me. then ah por cough also can cure. also make money
so can have light in the house. then no need borrow candle from
jesus anymore.

RAIN

We live always with rain.

Soft rain. Hard, driving rain.
Rain which cools, annoys, drenches, surprises.
Unseasonable, untameable rain.

Rain that jabs down
with stiff fingers, provoking umbrellas;
rain you want to walk in,
holding your hands
to your hot face in relief.

Rain whose percussion
on the upturned palm of a leaf
is the sound of wings
flapping, ready to take off.

Rain a kind of voice.
Listening, you think *Rain*
in the language you speak
alone to yourself.

Rain that falls equally
on grass and concrete,
which lasts so many nights
your very dreams are of

rain, dark against grey stone,
the gravel drinking in
its intermittent poetry,

footsteps falling into place
beside the rhythm of water,
forming its own song
and singing of its own arrival.

Gift of rain. Summons of rain.
Rain everywhere, so common
it is tragic. Rain that we live
around, rain as pervasive
and invisible as love, rain
unlooked for, and never missed,
rain that we hide from
in glass and stone,
pretending life is elsewhere.

Rain the colour of ash,
that beats down like grief,
unkind rain at midnight
that slices the shape
of cold in the hearts
of servicemen on night patrol.

Rain that keeps us in our place,
tapping firmly on the flat tops
of our roofs to remind us
who we are.

The same rain
that used to soak my father
and grandfather as they worked

the long streets: Liang Seah,
Sungei, Rochor, Waterloo, Victoria

(and not the same)

Rain that will never make crops
grow, squandered rain, a
wealth of rain to bless the sprouted
heads of our buried dead.

Rain we forget has fallen freely
and will return without us
to the hovering sky.

Rain that we know will go on
long after we too dissolve
into figures of stone, row
            upon row, a city of rain.

TO GO TO S'PORE

After ZAGAJEWSKI's 'To Go to Lvóv'

To go to S'pore. Which station
for S'pore, if not in a dream, at dusk, when rain
glistens on chrome. When Mass Rapid
Trains and Light Rail Trains are borne
to all corners. To leave in a hurry for S'pore,
night and day, in August or in May, but early,
but only if S'pore exists, if it is to be
found within the bounds
of this island and not just
in the colour of my passport, of my smart card;
if the smell of raintrees after thunderstorm,
of angsana, of frangipani, still lingers
like fresh smoke; if the canals brim
and grumble like epithets in Hokkien, vanish
beneath ground. To pack up and go, to leave
and never look back, at 5 p.m. to cease
like shop windows, while beneath the whirl
of fans in coffee shops, geckos chatter
their politics. But the office tower rises, straight
as the law, and everyone standing
in its shadow, and a mop and bucket leaning
on window glass, and our dream which hadn't
come yet, only concrete, and litter-bins and the
rainbow pulse of new pubs set to music, the low
bass tremble of bumboats, rocking.
Always too much of S'pore, no one
could fathom the depths of its neighbourhoods,
walk the inside trails between each block and hear
the creak and hiss of each brick speaking, scalded
by sun, at night the city's muteness, the dead

stillness in Shenton Way unlike that of temples
where monks keep silence full of unseen rivers.
In Liang Seah street history spilled
in unlit stairwells and on window louvres
swinging and shutting by themselves, in china
blue ceramic tiles, in flour, in the smell of eggs,
the form of feathers plastering the walls, in green
muck collecting in rusty pipes, fronds growing
where laundry once sprouted and the streets
played percussion and the air singed, the procession
of the devout sang like kings of the world
toward the temple gates. People in such frantic joy
they didn't want to stay indoors. So much life
it burst and flooded every street, it cracked the sky in
thunder and fireworks, the new year lived over
and over. My granny as she stood at the window
calling for my father, dinner ready and
steaming in the evening light and neighbours
shouting from windows, watching out for
trouble and the next meal and nothing tentative
as hope. An uncle slaved himself blind
reading by candlelight, while my father was out
catching fireflies. The health inspector came
and my grandfather bought him a drink
and covered the cockroaches with his sole, and
got away with it. Even then
there was too much of S'pore, it overflowed
each drain, came down as rain, so much and yet

none; what was there spawned, grew, cut
into shape not without love and now the green
June springs from every square, verdant wigs
pulled over everything. Weeds, attap, kampong
and five-foot way fell away as the towers rose,
pushing out above the temples, people shuffled on,
handbags and wallets full of tomorrow,
and every estate growing into each other,
and everyone a leaseholder, and now in a hurry
to just go, and somewhere to come and go from,
S'pore tugged every which way,
S'pore clutched in the small palm of the sea,
becoming and flowing in like tears, tides, currents,
rivers run beneath the surface everywhere

THIRTEEN WAYS OF LOOKING AT A SNOWSCAPE

"Location (6)", HANS OP DE BEECK

I

Have we been here before?

II

botched climate planning
blue chip imagination
clearly not enough

III

O verily how great are the works of the Creator
He layeth barren the verdant plains, he leaveneth all colour
He bringeth down the crown of the proud birch
He stoppeth up the waters, yea even unto their deepest reaches
He causeth the very air to smoke and blur like a lamp put out
The might of the sun is as nothing to Him, nor the capricious breezes
Tremble ye who know not the name of the Maker

IV

24kg wood ash
48kg sawdust
35kg chalk
2kg volcanic sand
4L housepaint "Arctic White" (non-toxic, waterproof, EzyCoat)

5kg albino elephant bone
13kg fossilised dandruff
67kg talcum (Silky Smooth Baby Soft ™)
30kg milk powder
22kg salt
109kg flour
42kg instant mashed potato flakes
49kg coconut flakes
10kg melamine
3.14kg cocaine
900g Monosodium glutamate
May Contain Nuts

V

Not quite *aiyowishiboughtthatthickmerinowoolcardiganonsale*
but certainly *goodthingirememberedmyextrajumper* and perhaps
   even
aboutthesameastheofficeairconononarainyday or
   hokkaidowasmuchworseinspring1997
for those accustomed to *alwayslikethatthenhavetoroadmarch* or
   thisiswhyiwanttoemigrate
in *diewaitkenaheatstroke* and *reallyfeellikehavingicekachang*
   conditions

VI

The hard September that broke my grandfather was worse than this
and it was only rain, premature and pitiless, daggerfuls of the stuff
coming down free of charge, rendering his whole naked lorryload
of rice worthless. Grandfather was a tough man, he'd outlived the

Japs, the Communists, he'd traded his pre-war fortune for a sore back and a labourer's diet, but this was the bayonet in the side, this was machine cruelty, and he said so in so many kicks to his ruptured, mudsucked tyres, breaking a toe in the telling of it. 六月雪, his wife my grandmother would have said. Snowfall in summer, downpour in dry heat, that operatic, cosmic signifier of a world gone awry, some terrible injustice done. He healed and fathered children who fathered children, lived to see them slush through decades of bewildering growth, a deluge of riches, his hair gone white in its proper time, a pipe in his mouth, more often than not, smoke-screened. Read the papers and took them lightly. Watched the sky for undue clouds.

VII

Are those rabbit ears
or the upturned feet
of a monk atoning
for treason?

VIII

In outer Cairo they met on the backs of camels approaching the desert, but in Tibet surefooted yaks were preferred when available. They timed their assignations to coincide with the Yangtze floods, and avoided solar eclipses except in Jutland. But here at last they could meet unaccosted by prying eyes for miles, veiled by the powdery fog in the shadows of bare trees, provided they were always careful to retrieve every scrap of clothing, and brush away their tracks, when they finally deigned to part.

IX

"Not here, Andre.
The blood will show for miles"

X

Afterwards
a prolonged and quiescent ceasefire
settled over the map
unchallenged

XI

silence as premonition:
the clean sheets
the intact branches
the prospect of thaw

XII

The first to go is your sense of place, and then of sense.
Dexterity declines, sight fades to blue, then white,
then darkens entirely. The memory of your first kiss
slips shyly out of view, and your mother's face follows, tsking.
The bullies grab their tawdry, empty schoolbags and trip
you one last time as they escape. Exeunt the seven cars you drove
and loved, the sixteen women who thought you were the one.

Farewell the coffeeshop on the corner of the narrow street,
the saltfish stench of passing bumboats on dark green rivers.
Every leaf on every tree fallen away long since, many more
than the days you remember, more than the days you forget.
Now you have shivered off your clothes, and now you are a mark
on the landscape, and now not even a mark. Turn over the white
    pages

XIII

always, a fresh canvas

LOADED

A close-up black and white photograph of a well-groomed, muscular groin, the American flag tattooed in colour just above the right pelvic bone. A fully erect penis, with the words "Fuck Iraq" graffittied along the shaft. You cannot picture it in your head without also conceiving of its obscenity. In that sense, it is a perfect marriage of form and content, medium and message.

* * *

Desirous of expressing her state of mind precisely, the Princess-Chancellor embroidered upon her inauguration gown the image of a butterfly caught in the faintest web of silk.

* * *

He takes the time to get his affairs in order. All his clothes, stuffed into a 28-inch suitcase, are left in locker 24 at the National Museum, the key consigned to the Chief Curator under the name of a famous guerrilla artist. The contents of his larder have been distributed across the soup kitchens on Plantation Road; his furniture broken down and reassembled as faux antiques bound for boutique hotels in Batan. His laptop, with all his secrets, is being couriered to an old lover in Hokkaido; any attempt to open a file would result in a botnet-borne bear run on the exchange. The incriminating manuscript and accompanying photographs, copied by hand, find their way to publishers both within and outside the regime under the guise of a cookbook. So he is able to finish one more cigarette, and admire the calligraphy of ant-trails on the ceiling, before the knocking comes, past midnight.

* * *

Every bullock sold, every slave redeemed, every barrel of grain emptied, all his material wealth entrusted to the safety of gold. It took a week to find him at the bottom of the murky reservoir, gleaming.

* * *

For the third session, she had them commit beautiful, ritual suicide. Enrolment resumed the next week. Classes were paid for in advance. At the fourth session she brought in guest speakers: past students, teleconferencing from the afterlife. Forget art, they advised. Live your life like the flame and the dance. It is what gives the hellbent their succour, and the heavenbound patience to endure eternity.

* * *

You misunderstand the gift, he cautions, with the patience of one who had outspoken death, arms aloft and apart, two bare feet set firmly on thin air. These wounds of mine are now your wounds. Flesh of my flesh, the fever in my blood will be your fever too. It will not be our selves, but our shadows that will conquer time.

* * *

However carefully he tried to crease or stiffly press the paper cranes, they soon crumpled under the steady rain. He left them on the temple steps nevertheless, trusting a Goddess of sufficient potency and inclination to read the firm and fervent prayer within the sodden mess.

* * *

It is time to ask yourself where your loyalties lie, she whispers, as she points the revolver at your temple, unfastens your robe and beckons you to the giant screen, while behind you the chanting rises to a frantic pitch.

UPGRADING

Give me more rooms, floor space, floors, dropped ceilings, cornices,
extra bathrooms, a toilet wide enough for a jacuzzi.

I want a kitchen I can fit an island in, stainless steel German cooker
hoods, state-of-the-art induction hobs even if I never use them.

Give me wall-to-wall parquet tiles, roman blinds, more curtains
than I'll ever open, so many square feet I won't have to knock down
a wall to make the place seem bigger. It IS bigger.

I want a bedroom so capacious I can park a Jaguar in it.

Two Jaguars. I want it large enough to be a local oddity, a tourist
attraction, the subject of awe and envy, a heritage site.

So huge, developers will knock on my heavy door, asking to turn
my land into condos for profit, and I will gleefully refuse.

I want it so generous friends would drive by and ask to drop off
their dogs for exercise runs.

I want a pad so massive I can go jogging in it and not get bored
with the view, so vast I can't see my neighbours without binoculars,
so tall I scan continents with my naked eye.

Of course a swimming pool. Make it Olympic-sized, lake-sized, a
body of clean water visible from space, one my father can go fishing
in any time he likes, a private indoor beach, like the one in Japan
with man-made waves, 2.5 metres high all year round.

Give me an estate so huge it'll be its own GRC. Heck, it'll have its own Parliament, a standing army, a separate time zone, the clocks always set to 6 p.m. on Sunday, the skies forever on the brink of twilight.

None of us will survive this anyway, says the flower, says the ant, whose abode is larger than any of ours.

So while we're at it, give me property with its own climate, the air tuned to a cool 23 degrees C, the clouds broadcasting jazz instead of rain.

And how about a mountain or two in the living room, each topped with ancient pines like overgrown bonsai. My own moon, that I can switch on or off with a flick of the wrist. A sun with a built-in dimmer. Stars to deck my Christmas forest with.

Rooms the size of night. Perfect quiet. Space at last to dream of islands without end.

MADE OF GOLD

> "The villagers were told that if they put their hands on the walls of
> Tekka market, money will flow out."
>
> *The Straits Times,* August 23, 1998

This too, is an image of ourselves:

walls that bleed money.
Dusty streets lined with gold.
Wave after wave, a babel sea
of dreamers on our shores. They build
our towers like cliffs, strong
against the sky. They build our homes
and our temples. In return
we lead them to our gods. Some are blessed.
Others learn to stretch a day's pay
for weeks, to be looked oddly upon
without flinching, to eat
with cracked hands.

> *First they take all my money.*
> *Then they take me to JB in lorry*
> *later go Singapore in tour bus.*
> *I hide in luggage hole with five others.*
> *I scared. They just push us in like that.*
> *Now I know they crooks but too late.*
>
> *I cannot go back they kill me I owe so much.*
> *I cannot pay back enough. Agent take my passport*
> *then dump me on streets of Tekka. I wash*
> *dustbin I scrub dump I sleep sometimes I eat.*

This all I got after working a
year. If only someone told
me the walls of Tekka
not made of gold.

62

lay out the dead, but do not mourn them overmuch.

a mild sentimentality is proper. nostalgia will be expected on demand.

cremate: conserve land, regret no secrets. prepare ashes for those with cameras.

hide your best furniture. tear down monuments. first to go are statues with arms outstretched in victory, and then anything with lions.

it is safer to consort with loss, to know the ground yet suggest no mysteries.

purport illiteracy.

have at hand servants good with numbers. err in their favour between schemes.

keep all receipts out of sight. as soon as is proper, embrace their laws and decline all credit for your own.

confound their historians. give up the wrong recipe for ketupat, for otak.

lay claim to the tongue of roots, the provenance of trees. when the chiku blooms, tell them it is linden. when linden, tell them it is ginko.

recommend laxatives as love potions. attribute pain to the passage of hard feelings. there will be a surge

of interest in soothsaying. do not tell them how it will end, or when. progress, while difficult, is always being made.

on no account acknowledge what your folktales imply.

never deal in the dark unless you can see the whites of their eyes.
when they speak of god

bow your head to veil piety, shame, laughter, or indifference.

dress your children like their long-dead elders. marry your daughters
to them.

soon you will attend the same funerals.

ACKNOWLEDGEMENTS

'Initiation', 'Fly-fishing', 'Friction' and 'Rain' were published in the collection *Testing the Silence* (Ethos Books, Singapore, 1996).

The following poems appear in the collection *City of Rain* (Ethos Books, Singapore, 2003): 'The Scent of the Real', 'Homecoming', 'Shades of Light in Holland Village', 'What to Write About in Cold Storage, circa 2000 AD', 'Absences', 'Poem for an Engineer', 'Merlign', 'The Meaning of Wealth in the New Economy', 'Salt', 'The Burning Room', 'Incendium Amoris', 'Rain', 'To Go to S'pore', 'Upgrading', and 'Made of Gold'.

'Patience' appears in *What Gives Us Our Names* (Math Paper Press, Singapore, 2011).

The following new and uncollected poems were completed with the support of the Arts Creation Fund (National Arts Council, Singapore): 'What it Means to be Landless', 'Other Things', 'Aubade', 'Candles', 'Thirteen Ways of Looking at a Snowscape', 'Loaded', and 'When the Barbarians Arrive'. Some of these poems have appeared in various journals and anthologies, including: *91st Meridian, Ars Aeterna, Australian Poetry Journal, Cha, Double Skin: New Poetic Voices from Italy and Singapore, Drunken Boat, Kontur, Over There: Poems from Singapore and Australia, Quarterly Literary Review Singapore, Salt Magazine, Tumasik: Contemporary Writing from Singapore, The Wolf* and others.

The author's profound thanks for making this collection possible are due to John Kinsella for his support, advice and energy, and to the tireless crew at Arc.

ALVIN PANG (b. 1972, Singpore) is a poet, writer, editor, anthologist and translator. His poetry has been translated into over fifteen languages and he has appeared in major festivals and anthologies worldwide.

A Fellow of the University of Iowa's International Writing Program (2002), his publications include *Testing the Silence* (1997), *City of Rain* (2003), *What Gives Us Our Names* (2011) and *Other Things and Other Poems* (Brutal: Croatia, 2012).

The anthologies he has curated include *No Other City: The Ethos Anthology of Urban Poetry* (2000); *Over There: Poems from Singapore and Australia* (co-edited with John Kinsella, 2008); and *Tumasik: Contemporary Writing from Singapore* (Autumn Hill, USA, 2009).

He is a founding director of The Literary Centre, a non-profit initiative promoting interdisciplinary capacity, multilingual communication, and positive social change. Among other public engagements, he is presently the managing editor of an internationally-circulated public policy journal. Pang was named the 2005 Young Artist of the Year for Literature by Singapore's National Arts Council, and was conferred the Singapore Youth Award (Arts and Culture) in 2007.

Also available in the Arc INTERNATIONAL POETS
series:

LOUIS ARMAND (Australia)
Inexorable Weather

DAVID BAKER (USA)
Treatise on Touch

ALISON CROGGON (Australia)
The Common Flesh

SARAH DAY (Australia)
New & Selected Poems

KEKI DARUWALLA (India)
The Glass-Blower: Selected Poems

GAIL DENDY (South Africa)
Painting the Bamboo Tree

ROBERT GRAY (Australia)
Lineations

MICHAEL S. HARPER (USA)
Selected Poems

SASKIA HAMILTON (USA)
Canal

ALAMGIR HASHMI (Pakistan)
The Ramazan Libation

DENNIS HASKELL (Australia)
Samuel Johnson in Marrickville

DINAH HAWKEN (New Zealand)
Small Stories of Devotion

BRIAN HENRY (USA)
Astronaut
Graft

RICHARD HOWARD (USA)
Trappings

T. R. HUMMER (USA)
Bluegrass Wasteland

ANDREW JOHNSTON (New Zealand)
The Open Window
Sol

JOHN KINSELLA (Australia)
Comus: A Masque
America (A Poem)
Lightning Tree
The Silo: A Pastoral Symphony
The Undertow: New & Selected Poems
Landbridge: An Anthology of
Contemporary Australian Poetry
ED. JOHN KINSELLA

PATRICK LANE (Canada)
Syllable of Stone

ANTHONY LAWRENCE (Australia)
Strategies for Confronting Fear

THOMAS LUX (USA)
The Street of Clocks

J.D.McCLATCHY (USA)
Division of Spoils

SELINA TUSITALA MARSH (Aotearoa / Samoa)
Fast Talking PI

TRACY RYAN (Australia)
Hothouse

MARY JO SALTER (USA)
A Kiss in Space

ELIZABETH SMITHER (New Zealand)
A Question of Gravity

C. K. STEAD (New Zealand)
Straw into Gold
The Right Thing
Dog

ANDREW TAYLOR (Australia)
The Stone Threshold

Lightning Source UK Ltd.
Milton Keynes UK
UKHW010627161120
373476UK00001B/52